Away on a Hilltop

The Continuing Story of the Manger Baby

Written by Gary Bower

Illustrated by Jan Bower

Storybook Meadow Publishing
Traverse City, Michigan

Published by Storybook Meadow Publishing, 7700 Timbers Trail, Traverse City, Michigan 49685.

www.GaryBower.com   www.JanBower.com

ISBN-13: 978-1-7321629-1-4   Printed and bound in Canada

Away in a

manger,

no crib for a bed,

the little Lord Jesus

laid down His sweet head.

The stars in the sky

looked down where He lay.

The little Lord Jesus

asleep on the hay.

Read Luke 2:1-7

Away in a

village

with carpenter's tools,

the growing Lord Jesus

observed all the rules.

His neighbors could see

that at work or at play,

the growing Lord Jesus

was quick to obey.

Read Matthew 13:55; Luke 2:39-40

Away in the

temple,

discussing God's Word,

the twelve-year-old Jesus

amazed all who heard.

His parents stood watching

with tears in their eyes.

The twelve-year-old Jesus

was thoughtful and wise.

_____

Read Luke 2:41-52

Away in a
river,

with crowds looking on,

the righteous Lord Jesus

was baptized by John.

A pure, gentle dove

settled down from the sky.

The righteous Lord Jesus

had pleased the Most High.

Read Matthew 3:13-17; Mark 1:9-11; Luke 3:21-22;
John 1:29-34

Away in the

wilderness,

hungry and thin,

the holy Lord Jesus

resisted all sin.

The evil one offered Him

riches and bread.

The holy Lord Jesus

chose God's way instead.

Read Matthew 4:1-11; Mark 1:12-13; Luke 4:1-13

Away on a

hillside

as people drew near,

the patient Lord Jesus

told all who would hear

great stories of faith

and His kingdom above.

The patient Lord Jesus

taught lessons of love.

Read Matthew 5, 6, 7 & 13; Luke 8, 12, 13, 14 & 15

Away on a

seashore,

much pain in the land,

the caring Lord Jesus

extended His hand.

The sick He would heal,

and the poor He would feed.

The caring Lord Jesus

helped people in need.

Read Matthew 4:18-25; Mark 6:53-56; Luke 8:26-56; John 6:1-13

Away to the
city
on Passover week,

the famous Lord Jesus

rode gentle and meek.

The people waved branches.

"Hosanna!" they cried.

The famous Lord Jesus

was known far and wide.

Read Matthew 21:1-11; Mark 11:1-10; Luke 19:28-41; John 12:12-19

Away in an

upper room,

leaving His seat,

the humble Lord Jesus

washed twelve pairs of feet.

His silent example

rang out through the hall.

The humble Lord Jesus

was servant of all.

Read John 13:1-17

Away in a

garden

of anguish and fright,
the kneeling Lord Jesus
prayed into the night.
The Father sent angels
to comfort His Son.
The kneeling Lord Jesus
prayed, "Your will be done."

Read Matthew 26:36-56; Mark 14:32-50; Luke 22:39-53

Away to a

council,

unjustly accused,

the sinless Lord Jesus

was beaten and bruised.

With silence He answered

each sinister lie.

The sinless Lord Jesus

was sentenced to die.

Read Matthew 26:57-27:31; Mark 14:53-15:20;
Luke 22:54-23:25; John 18:1-19:16

Away on a

hilltop,

no friends at His side,

the suffering Lord Jesus

so willingly died.

The darkness looked down

on the earth in its loss.

The suffering Lord Jesus

hung still on a cross.

Read Matthew 27:32-56; Mark 15:21-41; Luke 23:26-49; John 19:17-37

Away in a

graveyard

of sorrow and gloom,

the broken Lord Jesus

lay wrapped in a tomb.

When women came weeping

with perfume and prayer,

the body of Jesus

was no longer there.

Read Matthew 27:57-28:15; Mark 15:42-16:11;
Luke 23:50-24:12; John 19:38-20:18

Away to a

doorway

secured by a lock,

the risen Lord Jesus

did not have to knock.

His friends fell before Him

in shock and surprise.

The risen Lord Jesus

appeared to their eyes.

Read Mark 16:14; Luke 24:36-45; John 20:19-29

Away on a
cloud,

with His friends gazing high,

the glorious Lord Jesus

soared up through the sky.

The angels said, "Spread this

good news to all men:

The glorious Lord Jesus

is coming again!"

_____

Read Mark 16:19; Luke 24:50-52; Acts 1:7-11

God's Promise to Me

Away in His **kingdom** of pleasures unknown,
my wonderful Savior now sits on His throne.
And I am invited to join Him someday.
My wonderful Savior has paid for my way!

My Prayer to God

Away, **wash away** all my sin and my pride.
Forgive me, Lord Jesus, and clean me inside.
I trust what Your life-changing power can do.
Please save me, Lord Jesus. I'm calling on You.

The Bible Says:

"...This (Jesus) is the Lamb of God who takes away the sin of the world." (John 1:29)
"Everyone who calls on the name of the Lord (Jesus) will be saved." (Acts 2:21)

See more books by Gary & Jan Bower at
www.BowerFamilyBooks.com